Holidays and Celebrations
Halloween

by Brenda Haugen
illustrated by Sheree Boyd

Thanks to our advisers for their expertise, research, and advice:

Alexa Sandmann, Ed.D., Professor of Literacy
The University of Toledo, Toledo, Ohio
Member, National Council for the Social Studies

Susan Kesselring, M.A., Literacy Educator
Rosemount-Apple Valley-Eagan (Minnesota) School District

PICTURE WINDOW BOOKS
MINNEAPOLIS, MINNESOTA

For RaeLynn and Tylor. I love you so much it's scary!

Managing Editor: Bob Temple
Creative Director: Terri Foley
Editor: Sara E. Hoffmann
Editorial Adviser: Andrea Cascardi
Copy Editor: Laurie Kahn
Designer: Melissa Voda
Page production: The Design Lab
The illustrations in this book were rendered digitally.

Picture Window Books
5115 Excelsior Boulevard
Suite 232
Minneapolis, MN 55416
1-877-845-8392
www.picturewindowbooks.com

Printed in the United States of America.

Library of Congress Cataloging-in-Publication Data
Haugen, Brenda.
Halloween / by Brenda Haugen ; illustrated by Sheree Boyd.
p. cm. — (Holidays and celebrations)
Summary: Briefly discusses the history and customs connected to the celebration of Halloween.
Includes bibliographical references.
ISBN 1-4048-0195-2
1. Halloween—Juvenile literature. [1. Halloween. 2. Holidays.] I. Boyd, Sheree, ill. II. Title.
III. Holidays and celebrations (Picture Window Books)
GT4965 .H37 2004
394.2646—dc2   2003006103

Costumes, candy, and fun mixed with fright—
all these things make up Halloween.

Do you know why we celebrate Halloween?

The United States

Halloween is one of
the oldest holidays.
Its traditions come
from people who
lived long ago in
Ireland, England,
and other countries.

These people held fall festivals.
They celebrated the harvest
of their crops. They also
remembered those who had died.

Ireland

England

France

Portugal

Spain

Africa

7

Halloween was a scary day, too. These people believed in bad spirits. They wore costumes to scare away witches and goblins.

They were also very religious. Halloween began as a Christian holiday. The Christian church chose November 1 as All Saints' Day. The day before, October 31, was called All Hallows' Eve. All Hallows' Eve soon became known as Halloween.

October

	1	2	3	4	5	6
7	8	9	10	11	12	13
14	15	16	17	18	19	20
21	22	23	24	25	26	27
28	29	30	31			

November

				1	2	3
4	5	6	7	8	9	10
11	12	13	14	15	16	17
18	19	20	21	22	23	24
25	26	27	28	29	30	

In the 1800s, many people from Ireland and England moved to the United States and Canada. They shared their Halloween traditions. One tradition was to walk from house to house asking for food. Today, children go from house to house asking for candy. This is called trick-or-treating.

13

The Irish and English dressed up
in scary costumes. They told spooky tales.

They carved vegetables and put candles
inside to make lanterns.

Now, many people carve pumpkins on Halloween. They also dress up in costumes—but the costumes are not always scary.

Halloween includes many symbols.
Black cats and bats are Halloween symbols.
So are witches, ghosts, and skeletons.

People once thought witches could turn themselves into cats!

Black and orange are Halloween colors. Black stands for night. Orange is the color of fire. It also is the color of pumpkins!

Sometimes people make big outdoor fires on Halloween. These big fires are called bonfires. Long ago, people lit bonfires to scare away bad spirits.

19

When you go trick-or-treating,
you are part of the Halloween tradition.

So dress up in a costume. And don't forget to carve a jack-o'-lantern!

You Can Make a Halloween Mask

What you need:

crayons or markers
paper plate
scissors

hole punch
yarn

What you do:

1. Make sure you have an adult to help you.
2. Draw a jack-o'-lantern's mouth, eyes, and nose on the back of the paper plate.
3. Cut out the mouth, eyes, and nose.
4. Decorate the plate using crayons or markers.
5. Punch a hole on the right and left sides of the mask.
6. Cut a piece of yarn. Make sure that the yarn is long enough to hold your mask in place. Also make sure that you leave a little extra yarn for tying the two ends to the mask.
7. Thread the yarn through one of the holes on the side of the mask. Tie it. Thread the other end of the yarn through the hole on the other side of the mask. Tie it so that the mask fits securely.
8. Now your mask is ready to wear.

Fun Facts

- Halloween is celebrated in many countries, including the United States, Canada, Ireland, Wales, England, and Scotland.

- The first Halloween celebration in the United States took place in Anoka, Minnesota, in 1921.

- Some children trick-or-treat for the United Nations Children's Fund (UNICEF). They collect money that goes to help children who are poor and hungry.

- October 31 is a special day for magicians. It is National Magic Day. National Magic Day celebrates a famous magician named Harry Houdini.

Words to Know

bonfire—a big fire built outside

harvest—the gathering of crops

jack-o'-lantern—a carved pumpkin with a candle inside

spirit—a ghost

symbol—something that stands for something else

tradition—a belief or custom handed down from parents to children

trick-or-treating—going from door to door on Halloween to ask for treats

To Learn More

At the Library

Dickinson, Rebecca. **The 13 Nights of Halloween**. New York: Scholastic Inc., 1996.

Hintz, Martin and Kate. **Halloween: Why We Celebrate It the Way We Do**. Mankato, Minn.: Capstone Press, 1996.

Rau, Dana Meachen. **Halloween**. New York: Children's Press, 2001.

Silverman, Erica. **Big Pumpkin**. New York: Macmillan, 1992.

Van Straalen, Alice. **The Book of Holidays Around the World**. New York, Dutton, 1986.

Fact Hound

Fact Hound offers a safe, fun way to find Web sites related to this book. All of the sites on Fact Hound have been researched by our staff.

http://www.facthound.com

1. Visit the Fact Hound home page.
2. Enter a search word related to this book, or type in this special code: 1404801952.
3. Click on the FETCH IT button.

Your trusty Fact Hound will fetch the best sites for you!

Index

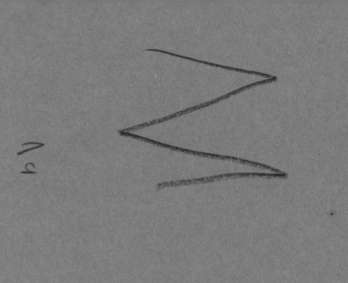